Through Her Eyes

Ashlee Nolan

BookLeaf Publishing

Presentation by *BookLeaf Publishing*

Web: www.bookleafpub.com

E-mail: info@bookleafpub.com

ISBN: 978-93-95223-13-3

First edition 2022

DEDICATION

I dedicate this book to all of those who struggle through this beautiful life journey with mental health and addictions. We will be the ones to change the world.

ACKNOWLEDGEMENT

I would like to acknowledge Jesus, as he is my #1, walking me through this process. I would like to acknowledge my son, Kayden, who gives me a reason to live. I thank my parents, Patrick and Kellie for bringing me into this world, and for never giving up on me. I would also like to thank my boyfriend, Shawn who was the first to read all of my poems. I would like to thank Bethesda Mission for supporting me and changing my life. I would like to thank all of those who helped me along the way. Finally, I would like to thank all of those who doubted me, told me no, and gave up on me. It's because of you that I am where I am today.

PREFACE

I started using drugs at the young age of 12. Before my active drug addiction came to an end at the age of 27, I lived a beautiful, yet disastrous life. My life was a roller coaster of emotions and events. Since I struggle with Borderline Personality Disorder, Bipolar Disorder, and ADHD, I needed a way to feel and express and to exist in this world that I could not define nor explain nor make sense of. I found relief through drugs alcohol and sex. Although I believe drugs helped me in the beginning, for an addict like me, in the end they took everything. Most importantly they took my mind, spirit, family, and relationship with God. I like to see things in an optimistic light, so I believe they gave me so much more. If I were to regret anything in my 31 years of life, I would not be right here right now writing this to you. I came to my senses November 30th, 2017 and realized I would never have the family I so very longed for if I kept living the way I was. Homeless, strung out, unhealthy, toxic, lost, confused, delirious, in fear of my own shadow. So I decided to get help. After a 4 month TC program and a 4 year Christian program, I am 4 and a half years clean off all drugs and alcohol. I am 2 and a half years cigarette free. I am in college studying Addiction & Recovery Services. I have a healthy relationship with my boyfriend. The first healthy relationship I've ever had. I have a relationship with my family and myself and most importantly Jesus. I find peace in words and rhyming and poetry. I write to escape, yet I somehow always find my way back to myself. I also write in hopes to relate to others who are also at a loss for words.

Lately

Lately I've been thinking,
Well actually I think a lot.
I'm glad I'm no longer using drugs or drinking,
Yeah during them days I was in a bad spot.
I didn't know I had an addiction.
I didn't know the true problem.
I didn't know I've been gifted,
With not knowing how to solve them.
I thought I had it all figured out.
I was going to change the world.
What I really had was fear and doubt.
I was a scared, lost little girl.
I lived in this world that I created.
It only made sense in my mind.
Whether high or not I was faded.
I really had a whole world left to find.
I was blind.
Living life by pressing forward and then rewind.
Stuck in the moment,
Trapped in the grind.
I feared to fail,
Yet I failed to fear.
Only when the drugs were near,
Did anything seem clear.

My perception was clouded by the reality I
wanted near.
Not knowing what I truly wanted,
I became the ghost who I haunted
Running from the law,
All I had to do was fall.
But I was scared to lose it all.
All of what I didn't have left.
Not knowing what was to come next.
I knew I wanted to be better at life.
So I got clean that night

Kayden

I never knew how much love my heart could
hold until I carried you.
What to do, I had no clue.
Weeks went by and the years they flew.
In my life God designed a picture, you were the
chosen one he drew.
As moments pass by. I sometimes wonder why
he chose me to give you life.
Our love is something I will hold onto with all
my might.
Situations may seem like a constant fight.
Sometimes we may battle whether we're wrong
or right.
Someday you'll understand why the angels
haven't left your sight.
Whenever you feel scared, just open up and
write.
Getting your thoughts out may feel like stress at
first,
But when you're done you'll feel relaxed just like
after, to you I gave birth.
Just always remember, you my son have worth.
Endless to be exact.
You can be anything you want to in this world
and that's a fact.

So stand your ground.
Don't ever forget how much you make me
proud.
Know that I will always be around.
How does that sound?
It's you Kayden Patrick that I absolutely adore.
To give my life for you, this I swore.
And I will always do all I can to give you more.

Love

They say love is patient and love is kind,
Why does it look so different inside my mind?
Why do I want what I can't have?
Yet get attached to what I attract?
I hear, when you know you know.
Is that why, to me, you feel like home?
A home I've never known.
A home to where I always wanted to go.
I guess I just have to give it time.
I don't want to speak too soon, but I feel like
you're already mine.
Although you don't belong to me, because you're
surely a gift from above.
I rarely get to see you.
I guess that's what you call blind love.
I don't know why I'm so stuck on you.
The way I feel about you, you probably have the
slightest clue.
What am I to do?
Why am I confused?
I just want you to want me.
I want what I perceive for you to see.
There's many others with whom I could be with.
But it'd be for you, if I had one wish.
I see so much potential inside of you.

I see you as a man that's nothing but true.
I feel such a strong urge just to be in your
presence.
Everytime I'm around you, I feel this intense
essence.
I love that you are a pure soul.
To give us a chance, is my goal.
I'll give you your space until you see what I do,
In hopes that one day, you'll love me too.

Mental State of Mind

It comes in different forms.
Imagine inside you there's a storm.
Into pieces you're being torn.
It's like something you can't explain.
Constantly going insane.
Feeling clouded in the brain.
Like a cartoon that falls from the sky.
You descend, yet your head stays up high.
You're always questioning why.
Over thinking yet under thinking.
Turning to drugs and drinking.
Waves in your brain just don't be linking.
Always wanting to please everyone.
Impulsive, yet never getting anything done.
It's like fighting a battle you have not won.
Feeling like you're out of your skin.
Spend your time walking a line that's thin.
Like sinking and not knowing how to swim.
I live in an alternate reality because I have
psychosis.
I have ADHD and tend to lose focus.
I battle with a thinking disorder, not knowing
how to control my emotions.
Don't get me wrong, there are ways to cope.
So don't ever lose hope.

Healing with every word that I wrote.
I've found other ways to express myself.
It is important to treat your mental health.
It's not always your fault for the cards you were
dealt.
Doing drugs can alter the chemicals in your
head.
And having imbalanced chemicals can cause
you to do drugs instead.
I've gotten alot of advice from all the books that
I've read.
Which is another way that I learn to heal.
It's okay to ask for help for you to deal.
I can relate to those who can't describe how they
feel.
I make it my mission to deliver a positive
message.
My whole life I've been learning a lesson.
I no longer have to suffer, which to me is a
blessing.

The Lotus That Grew From Mud

Are you still alive? I believe so.
I believe it was just your time to go.
To a place to be, an avenue to achieve.
It's like you're on the other side,
Where they told you that you died.
Yet this whole time you tried to hide,
Without getting blindsided by your pride.
So when was the last ride?
Or did it even yet take place?
I love the fact that we run the same race.
Our passion is on the same pace.
The memories flow through me like your love in
my veins,
The power of your spirit fills the holes in my
brains.
I'm closest to God when I'm closest to you.
The day I found you, was the day one was made
from two.
I don't know who you are, or if this even makes
sense.
I just know what I feel and that it's intense.
So when we say yes to each other, know it's for
good.

For from death to life we were raised up, just
like we should.

Wasted Space

There's so much I could be doing to work on
myself,
But instead I sit here crying out for help.
I have all the answers all around me,
Yet I refuse to dig inside to unlock what is meant
to be.
What I'm meant to see.
I just want to keep writing to let it all out,
And rhyming words without worrying about
how it all sounds.
When I'm asked questions that get me to think,
I'm left in a cloud of doubt, and I slowly start to
sink.
I give up on this ink.
There seems to be a missing link.
Like why am I doing this to begin with?
Or am I just wasting my time, avoiding what's
amidst?
I guess time's not wasted, because it all has a
purpose.
I just know in order to heal, I need to get past
this future's presenting surface.
Maybe that's what I'm doing by writing this here
script.
I wonder, will I ever catch my drift?

I don't use my time wisely or do I?
Atleast I'm no longer doing things that put me at
risk to die.
You see, before, I always put myself in the
position to be high.
Because it was then that I thought I had the best
to say, and I don't know why.
Everything is simple sober, and it seems no
longer deep.
I miss using the feelings I did when I would
weep.
The nights when I couldn't sleep.
I was okay with not eating for a week.
I was weak,
Far from meek.
I was looked at as a freak.
My life was bleak.
I was worried about changing the world
But not the fact that I was still a twenty
something year old little girl.
I tried to take the job of the Lord,
And ended up at the devil's door.
I even tried to take on his job, the most evil of
spirits.
Because I tried to live backwards, like those
lyrics.
I fell asleep while I was awakened to someone
else's dreams.
And then I pressed repeat,

On the past of someone else's future present of
me.

Life as She Knew it

Chaos and confusion or was that just going on
inside of me,
Happy go lucky or was that just what only I
could see.
Beautiful disaster was the life that I was after.
I don't know why I saw hell as heaven,
I don't know why to me a good sign is seven
seven seven.
I just see life differently.
I guess you could say I've gained some clarity.
But I haven't always been this way.
I can't tell if I have more or less to say today.
I've had to struggle most of my life. My best
learning was through lessons of Strife.
It's safe to say that I've awakened to reality.
The ignorance in this world is just so sad to see.
I'd rather think too much than not at all, the
world's greatest teacher was the fall.
I look at things from a metaphysical point of
view,
but you know what they say under the sun
there's nothing new.
I think we're always in a state of greater
becoming,
Funny how I got here was by me numbing.

The voices in my head can at times be too much,
maybe because Satan has that magic touch.
I've given my life to Christ and He's given me
reason to live,
When I was down on my luck and had nothing
else to give.
He just wanted my heart.
It had afterall been His from the start. I don't
know what my future holds.
It's not easy but it's worth it or so I've been told.
I just want to live to do the right thing,
And positively impact all the people that to me
he will bring.
I've learned to live my life one day at a time,
And wake up to write them down when in my
sleep I would rhyme lines. I know sometimes I
can be all over the place.
I know now that I can say thank God for his
grace.
I'd just like to show the world how I got through.
My life was a mess, yes it is true.
I destroyed every part of my entire being,
Turns out that being the life of the party was
totally deceiving.
I wanted to be somebody that I wasn't. To
survive I thought I needed joy in an over
abundance.
I didn't want to numb my feelings except for
pain,

Knowing that walking around a happy camper
was only living for everyone else's gain.
I did what I had to in order to survive, These
streets aren't your friend and in them you cannot
thrive.
I was looking for love in all the wrong places.
Inside of me is where I found that God's grace is.
I want to give back I just don't know how yet.
I'm glad I can look back on my life and say
there's nothing that I regret. Everything happens
for a reason if it didn't it wouldn't have
happened.
The whole time I was a crew member while He
was the captain.
I thought it was me that was totally in control.
Until I landed myself in that deep dark hole.
Survival mechanisms kicked in and told me the
only way out,
Was to believe in Him without a shadow of a
doubt.

Time

I never knew what it took to wait.
I now know what it means when they say, "it's
never too late."
It's like I had wrote to myself when I read what I
write,
Yet in the midst of the memory, I had only those
amongst insight.
When you ask God to control the door,
What are you banging on it for?
Praying he'd bring us closer together,
Asking if you're meant to be in my life forever.
Praying he'd tell you to kick rocks,
If you're just wasting the time on my clock.
Praying if we're not meant to be,
He'd kindly find a way for you to leave.
I almost have you, yet what good is that?
I need to know you got my back.
Has it been in my head all of this time?
They say follow your heart, but my love is blind.
I don't want to let go, but it seems you already
have.
I stay holding on to someone who doesn't want
grabbed.
Maybe it's just the distance.
We don't need all the resistance.

I'm just all about persistence.
Tell me, is there a mistress?
To God I got to listen.
There's alot to be risking.
For us there may be another
I love you enough to wait for you.
So for now let's release each other.

My Savior

Is my writing another form of a drug that I use?
To distract myself from all the abuse?
Is it healthy though, that is the question.
I guess that's the quest I'm on.
Repair my soul Lord.
Show me my purpose Lord.
I know there's more.
May the Holy Spirit guide me toward,
Everything that moves me forward.
I'm not going to find it in sex, drugs, money,
food, or them Father. I'm only going to find it in
you.
What am I to do?
I feel like I'm on the loose.
And everyone else is confused.
They won't listen to me,
Because I don't know how to speak.
They don't take me seriously,
Because I am weak.
Is this really the stuff inside that bothers me?
Help me escape all that encaptures me from
being free.
I don't want to escape, I want to go through it.
But only you God, I know that you can do it.

Unity

I just want to fly away to a place thats warm.
Where everyone is adorn.
And everyday we're reborn.
Where love comes first, not last.
And we're all together, yet on our own unique
individual paths.
Family means loyalty.
Christ is royalty.
Faith over hate.
There's hope,
To never again desire dope.
Endless chances are given and received.
There's nobody left to be deceived.
A place where dreams come true.
A place for me, a place for you.
The wind blows ever so softly on your skin,
As soft as the heart that takes the time to listen.
Does such a place exist where great minds think
alike?
Where an idea we share and then don't have to
think twice.
Where trust is a must.
You won't need to finish my sentence for me,
Because words won't even be necessary.
But when we do speak to each other,

We can relate like no other.
We have fun in the sun.
Our kids run,
Wild young and free,
And can just simply be.
A place where everybody would give their all.
Nobody would have to fall.
A spot to belong,
Where it's okay to be wrong.
There's no room for war, because there's too
much peace taking place.
There's no room for prejudice,
Because there's only one race.
Color isn't defined by our skin,
And money wasn't designated to our next of kin.
What if we lived in a world we all could share?
Where for once it all was fair.
Equal love for all of us.
Leave alone the hate for once.
What it would be like to live in a world where
we actually had a chance.
A chance to be happy.
To live not just survive.
To thrive.
To be important.
To be healthy
To have everything you need.
To go to school.
To have a home.

To no longer be alone.
What if the world could change?
I live in a world where I want to live in a
different world that remains in my brain.

My First Born

My first born.
Without you I am torn.
I think of all the excuses in the universe,
Why not to go in depth about our estranged
relationship, and how I want that to be reversed.
On my life there was this curse,
With us from birth.
But things changed for the better.
Those chains were severed.
A long, long time ago in our family,
It wasn't meant for us to be.
Kids were taken,
If I'm not mistaken.
In order to get them back,
You had to prove what you did lack.
It only seemed fair,
That the parents would have to share.
Back then the jury's been spoken
Our family genes were just meant to be broken.
Not forever says the Lord.
For one day a holy family we could afford.
It's true when they say talk is cheap.
We really do sow what we reap.
Everyone on both sides of my family at one
point lost their kids,

As if their next of kins came with directions.
Our parents got their moral compasses from
their parents.
So on and so forth was their inheritance.
It's nobody's fault in this world unknown.
You can only do what you've been shown.
In a fallen world I'm doing my best,
To make sure I turn it all over to God for all the
rest.
I believe that is my generational test.
Leading me to my family's nest.
When I found out I was pregnant I wasn't ready.
My son's father and I were barely going steady.
I had no idea that a decade later my life would
be like this,
At one point my mom, to my stomach, took her
fist.
She wished my son dead, I have no idea why.
Or did she understand the curse and not want to
have to lie?
Regardless, now I learn to forgive and move
forward.
Looking back at all aspects, I get what her anger
was toward.
There's a lot of hurt in my family and history
repeats itself.
But it doesn't have to, just cause life recycles it's
health.
My son was born perfectly fine.

I cannot believe something like this could be
mine.
I had no logic of a baby ten years ago
Or the gift of God they are, when all I wanted to
be was a hoe.
Kids don't come with instructions,
And when you don't take care of them there are
repercussions.
Mine came in the form of God taking him from
me.
To place with his father temporarily.
I wasn't the best mom, I didn't know how to be.
I put other people, places, and things before my
child and it took him being away for that I could
see.
My son was taken care of physically,
But emotionally he was deprived you see.
How could I take care of him when I couldn't
take care of me?
Psychologically I was withdrawn, and with a
child that's a dangerous place to be.
I was immature, I stopped developing at a young
age.
By going to court all the time, I felt like I lived
on a stage.
Nothing was healthy, except the love I had for
him,
Not even the place where it all begins.
So what do you do in that situation?

I left it to God without hesitation.
I made wrong choices which led up to the last
goodbye.
It's been so long I can't even cry.
It took almost ten years for me to realize why
my son wasn't here.
Having a child meant having no freedom, or so
it appeared.
I remember one day my son crying asking for
pappy,
I thought him going to live with his father and
grandparents would make him happy.
Never were my intentions to not get him back.
My son's dad kept him from me ever since then,
as a matter of fact.
I started spanking my son right before this time
which I never did.
This is the stuff in which I always hid.
I don't believe in hitting your kid.
I did it out of anger, whatever he did.
I knew at that point something had to change,
I didn't know however, I was mentally deranged.
I was just doing to him what was done to me,
Repeating the cycle, reliving history.
Regardless to what others do, I'm responsible for
my own,
Although on the inside a kid, outside I'm fully
grown.
I left my son's dad when he was a year old,

Scared I'd be judge, my story's been left untold.
I have an addiction that started as a child,
And as a teen I chose to be wild.
My son's father also addicted to drugs.
It's like my son was created by two closet thugs.
I knew I was done with his dad when I saw a
text from his friend,
Saying, "yo tomorrow can you hit me again?"
I went to check his arms only to find,
That for awhile he's had something to hide.
I told him if he didn't tell his family that I would,
Things just weren't going the way I thought they
should.
I told him I was leaving and taking our son,
The battle begun.
I took him with me and moved to another state.
I told his dad if he wanted to see him, he would
have to wait.
Until we got a court order and I knew he
couldn't keep him.
This is where hell begins.
We battled in court for about two years.
Finally I showed up and broke down in tears.
I didn't know how to fight anymore than I did,
I did the best I could and then I back slid.
On top of addiction I battle with my mental state
of mind.
I put this off for so long because it got thrown in
my face, anything that they could find.

Even after knowing my son's dad comes from a
similar background,
The judge found him to be more stable. And
those were just the facts now.
My son's father was fighting an addiction of his
own.
But he had a family and support that was shown.
Although I still have rights to our child,
My son has been kept from me for awhile.
I haven't had the means to fight for him since,
Seven years later, now that's a long length.
Kayden knows who I am and that I love him
very much.
It's just that I was so afraid to lose him that I lost
touch.
Not having him around affects my everyday,
And I know it affects him in every way.
God has a purpose for all of our lives.
Sooner rather than later, having him in my life is
what for I strive.
I'm scared to move forward and have anymore
kids,
Because of my past and all the things that I did.
If I knew how to be a mother I would have had
this thing covered.
Matter of fact I did,
But from responsibility I hid.
Before my son was here,
I was in a relationship for almost five years.

Long story short I lost all of my teens,
I still don't even know what love means.
I got it from all the wrong places.
I looked for it in pretty faces.
My step father was racist.
Which didn't mix well because my family is full
of mixed races.
I struggled on a day to day basis.
Always on probation with open cases.
Having the wrong idea of everything from things
to people to places.
So how do I express the love I have for my son?
When it seems as though I have love for no one.
I live my life to better it for me.
So that I can better each and every single seed.
Which includes him,
My next of kin.
One day he will be old enough that I can
elaborate on what has happened all this time,
And when that day comes I hope in his heart
forgiveness he can find.
What I pray the most is that this doesn't effect
his entire life.
That issues don't arise with his, one day, wife.
I pray that the cycle breaks with me,
And his children don't have to live a life, my
child had to see.

Confusion

It's like they already knew,
Everything she went through.
Just by the way that she drew.
And who she associated with as a crew.
Only a few knew the truth.
The reasons behind why she flew.
And how much she grew.
Understanding her takes more than what you
know.
More than whom she chose to show.
Or why she practices how to go with the flow.
A following was not her intent.
For she could talk to herself whenever she
wanted to vent.
Focusing on her words alone, making sure it's
what she meant.
It's not easy growing from cement
Alone without anyone knowing what she meant.
When she got tired of hearing "keep wishing,"
To change the world became her only mission.
Who knew they would,
She thought she could.
While others hid,
She actually did.

The Verge of Relapse

I feel stuck again,
Like I'm too broken to pay attention.
I stay distracted to keep myself from having to
deal with my feelings.
I'm aggravated with myself because I want to
produce.
Yet I refuse to let loose.
The thought of substances come to mind.
I feel like I need a substance of some kind.
To ignite the flame that's been put out.
To spark the light that's behind this cloud.
They say only the Holy Spirit can fill that.
And I believe that's true as a matter of fact.
So why do I feel like I lost it all when I lost the
drugs?
Losing those were worse than losing his hugs.
My brain went down the drain.
My spirit has been depleted.
Or is this just what's left after the beginning of
the end of me is completed?
It just doesn't make sense.
Why's everything so dense?
I just want to feel, this I confess.
I want to feel alive without having to get
undressed.

I want to laugh, to cry.
To do all the things I used to do, the things that
would make me ask why.
I'm sick and tired of being sick and tired.
Life's a full time job, yet I somehow still manage
to get fired.
All I know how to do is think.
It's surprising what ends up in ink.
I want to get better,
Most importantly I want to realize that I am
already doing my best.
I want to be a go getter,
But I want to, while I have the opportunity, to
take my time and get some rest.
One reason I feel so rough,
Is because I feel like I'm not doing enough.
As long as I do what I say I'm going to,
Than I won't put myself through what I have
brought myself to do.
You see what I mean,
Is I choose to stay clean.

Two of You

It's not fair to you,
That I can't choose between you two.
He doesn't even want me, and what's sad,
Is I fool myself into thinking he does and that's
bad.
Us being together was more than a fad.
You were the best thing I ever had.
Who am I even talking to anymore? You would
never know.
The feelings you have for me you boldly show.
You see I don't want to just fall back on you,
I'd want to make all your dreams come true.
With him I'm chasing a fantasy of what if.
A never have I ever if you catch my drift.
It's not just with him that it all makes sense,
Except the fact that I don't know if he wants me
and that's hard to accept.
I've been with you before and it hasn't worked
out.
The guy I marry I do not want to doubt.
And you both deserve women who know who
they want forsure,
So for now I'm going to stay alone, because my
love is immature.

Agape Love

Have you ever loved what you didn't like to see?
That's how agape love relates to me.
I used to be shy yet wise,
But I would despise guys if they weren't my
type.
Figuratively speaking,
Girls in my life were just not for the keeping.
Being a bi-sexual sex addict,
Staying close to anyone was a bad habit.
Girls were dramatic, deceptive, and lame.
Guys didn't run their mouth, liked to chill up in
the house, and I ran the same game.
When it came to love,
I didn't wear a glove.
My guidance came from above.
My visions were a few and far between.
If you can read between the lines you can hear
just what I mean.
To substantially sustain myself I had to use
substances to substitute each other,
When I was out of drugs I needed a lover.
My emotions came from potions.
Exploding oceans of overdoses.
Coast to coast I stayed in the same boat.
Looking for hope,

Thought I found it in dope.
So why was I in the streets do you ask me?
Because it beats having to be deceased by some preconceived
Notions of misconceived motions, deceived devotions.
Love lost was at one point Love found,
Which means Love was to come back around.
You fail to see what you don't care for,
And don't care to see what might make your soul soar.
Try to see past the last that stabbed you in the back.
The more hate you carry around,
The more you discriminate and it's bringing you down.
Learn to love yourself first,
That's natural from birth.
Somewhere down the line we learned behaviors.
Behaviors that were major.
Teaching us ways we needed to be in order to receive.
Then we grew up with or without plenty, instead of healthy roots we had weeds.
Instead of growing gardens, we're planting these seeds.
We fail to see what we used to survive.
We need food, blood, oxygen to thrive.
We also need love.

But we don't need to do anymore than be
ourselves in order to receive some.
Learning to love others naturally,
Is really not what it's all masked up to be.
When you block others out,
You box yourself in without a doubt.
So how do I apply agape love to my life?
By believing in the opposite of Strife.
In hopes of one day becoming a wife.

Another Kind of Drug

I like going to sleep,
So that I can dream.
In which I escape reality,
Somewhere I go that's deep.
Either way there's an in between,
Like reverse psychology.
I'm hanging it up, I overflow my cup.
Pictures on the wall splatter paint trays of minds
eyes yet to be saw.
A puzzle yet to be solved.
When art is involved,
My soul is resolved.
My time has been called,
Out of here I'm hauled.
Off of it I'm walled.
Yet still I'm awakened while I am under,
Consciously unconscious in a subconscious
slumber.
Away from the present I slip,
Past the future, now that's a gift.
At myself I have to laugh,
Because I'm back towards the present I first
stopped at last.
And moving forward the future is presented in
the past.

Whatever it takes to avoid making mistakes.
That is the game I'm not trying to play.
What if the world could change in a day?
What if the words didn't interfere with the
meaning of what I say?
What if I woke up right now and just said "I'm
okay?"
Am I even here or in this bed do I still lay?
I don't know anymore, because I'm in my own
way.

Healing

It's like I try to hurt myself just so I can feel,
Why's it gotta be pain just for me to deal?
I think of all the bad just to keep it real,
Any memory it would take just so I would heal.
I use the same words over and over again,
Just to put me in a different position, than I was
in before then.
I remember when I didn't have holes on my
brain,
I forget that healed I'm still completely insane.
My body hurts, my minds confused.
My souls been scourned, my spirit's bruised.
Wondering if I will ever change anything to
make it last,
Or will it all remain just like in the past?
Addictive sounds so descriptive.
Reminds me of why I'm so gifted,
Yet I stay feeling convicted.
Locked in chains,
My mind is set in ways.
Everyday is like a game.
Is it the same or is it deranged?
I think I've been framed.
I'm sick of being the same.

My father says I have to be tired in order to be
tamed.
I like to sleep,
But resting is too deep.
As I reach my main peak,
I feel the enemy come in between.
A new me I seek.
That's why I have to hold onto the image of the
proof.
Jesus died for you, no need to feel ashamed of
his name.
His grace made us free, so he is to blame.

Stressed Out

If everything is temporary, why has it been so
long?
If everything happens for a reason, why does it
feel so wrong?
It's like I can't be used,
Until the producer says it's time to be produced.
I don't want to start a fight,
Yet if I stay I might.
Back and forth toss and turn,
I guess that's the spot I earned.
It's hard to move forward when I'm always
looking back,
And I'm steady looking toward whatever I lack.
I don't reach out for support and help,
Even though for it I cry and I yelp.
I feel like I'm at the bottom line,
And I stay there acting like I'm fine.
Deep inside it hurts,
All the chaos is worse.
It's like the hole is too deep to climb out,
And I live on the edge with fear and doubt.
Today I feel like I'm flat lined trying to raise the
bar,
I don't know why it is but should it really be this
hard?

My emotions don't flow free anymore,
I can barely get up off the floor.
I want to be free, I want to fly, I want to touch
the sky.
I didn't think I had a choice,
Out here lost without a voice.

Change

Today is unseen,
Tomorrow is just a dream,
Yesterday is a mystery,
All we have is the in between.
Either way I'm going to survive,
Do you want to know why?
Because I'm not in these streets trying to get
high.
Looking for ways out, just letting me die.
I know you're tired, but you just have to do it,
Go out there and show them this is music.
Sometimes it feels like you have to prove it,
But know that we all really go through it.
I used to think that telling the truth one time was
enough,
Well I'm going to call my bluff.
There's layers that you have to peel,
Situations that you have to deal,
I'm finally getting the chance to heal.
Do you think we can just change over night?
If we could, would you be my next reason to
write?
Always rushing next season to flight,
With no end in sight,
And when any change occurs we put up a fight.

What's the use in staying stuck in a rage?
I can't get off this page,
Ending up in a cage,
Frightened on stage,
Why stay stuck in this place?
Still on this phase,
When you can change your ways,
There is only one lane.
Just be careful what you pick,
Some decisions truly stick,
And always remember that secrets keep you
sick.

Sick and Tired

Sitting here reminiscing,
About the things I've been missing.
Looking back at the past,
Oh how I wanted it to last.
But I could get it all back,
Minus the drugs and the weapons,
Prosecutors and defendants,
Fakes and pretenders.
A life without crime,
I don't want to do the time.
I've made my decision,
Everything could be different,
I don't want to go to prison.
My life flashed before me,
A life I don't want my kids to see.
I pray for better days,
First I have to change my ways.
So on to the next chapter,
A new life I am after.
Tired of losing my soul,
It's time to take control.
So what am I going to do?
When I don't have nothing to prove.
I just don't want to lose.
Jesus Christ I do choose.

He saved my life.
One day I want to be a wife.
And get my son back,
I have to pick up my own slack.
For some things I do lack.
I want to build a house,
My home I had to re-route.
It's not time to resurrect,
I have to take care of what I neglect.
And earn back my respect.
A true story's what I claim,
I'll take that to my grave.
Yes the truth hurts,
On my life was a curse,
But then I put it in reverse,
It's not my time to be in a hearse.
I love my family,
To see them stay alive is not a guarantee.
So I pray a lot,
Try to put them in the right spot.
That curse I did stop,
I'm going to make it to the top.
This is how I want to end it,
My second chance is now blended.

The Journey

I used to get high,
At times I wanted to die.
She lost her way and wondered why at times she
did lie,
She stayed away, because it was bard to say
goodbye.
She turned her life around,
He picked her up when she was down.
No clowning around,
No reason left to frown.
It's been years since, in her tears, she used to
drown.
Jesus was the one to save me,
No ifs ands buts or maybes.
No longer was she crazy.
Her life's been rearranged,
At times she may seem strange,
But no longer is she deranged.
She has an addictive personality,
Alot of people doubted me,
But you say that you're proud of me.
Today life is different,
No longer am I a mistress.
I abuse my body less,
Because of this I'm blessed.

I turn the speakers up,
When I've had enough.
A wise woman once told me that music
entertains,
You should see what she comes up with, you
would be amazed.
I now see better days,
No longer is my world in haze,
It's only because of God's grace.
She has a son,
In whom she loves.
He was sent from up above,
For him she'd give her life if push came to
shove.
She's extremely proud of him,
Being a good mother comes from within.
She loves her family,
Nowadays this is clear to see.
She wants to inspire others,
So they don't grow up like her mother.
There was a curse on her family tree,
But one day God spoke to me.
Baby girl you've had enough,
This time I'm calling Satan's bluff.
Your prayers have succeeded,
No longer is a curse needed.
Now I can be an example for the rest to see,
You can do it just look at me.
There's no better place to be,

Thanks to being drug free.
I can now live beyond my wildest dreams.
Captivate my mind, unleash my spirit.
When I look at you, I know you are nearest.
She's changed her ways,
God paved her lane,
He's made a way,
Because now she's saved.